ECLECTIC EDUCATIONAL SERIES.

M^CGUFFEY'S

SECOND

ECLECTIC READER.

REVISED EDITION.

ECLECTIC EDUCATIONAL SERIES.

M^cGUFFEY'S

SECOND

ECLECTIC READER.

REVISED EDITION.

NEW YORK ❖ CINCINNATI ❖ CHICAGO

AMERICAN BOOK COMPANY

ISBN 978-1-4341-0517-2

Published by Waking Lion Press, an imprint of the Editorium.

The Editorium, LLC
West Jordan, UT 84081-6132
www.editorium.com

PREFACE.

In this book, as well as in the others of the Revised Series, most of the favorite drill selections, which constituted one of the leading excellences of McGuffey's Readers, have been retained. New selections have been inserted only when they seemed manifest improvements on those formerly used.

The plan of this Reader is a continuation and extension of that pursued in the First Reader.

If the pupil is not familiar with the diacritical marks, he should be carefully drilled, as suggested on page 7, until the marked letter instantly suggests the correct sound. He is then prepared to study his reading lessons without any assistance from the teacher.

All new words are given at the head of each lesson. When these are mastered, the main difficulties left for the pupil are those of expression. In the latter portion of the book the simpler derivatives,—such as are formed by adding one or two letters,—possessives, plurals, verbal forms, etc.,—are omitted if the primitive word has been given. In this way the pupil is gradually led to the mastery of words as ordinarily printed.

A few of the most usual abbreviations have been introduced,—such as Mr., Mrs., etc. These should be carefully explained, not only as to their meaning and use, but as to the reason for their use.

Great care has been taken to have the illustrations worthy of the reputation M^CGUFFEY'S READERS have attained, and some of the foremost designers of this country have contributed to the embellishment of the book.

Many of these pictures will serve admirably for lessons in language, in extension and explanation of the text. The imagination of the artist has, in some cases, filled in details not found in the text.

The thanks of the publishers are due to very many experienced teachers, who have contributed their valuable suggestions.

June, 1879.

CONTENTS

ARTICULATION.

SUGGESTIONS TO TEACHERS.—Thorough and frequent drills on the elementary sounds are useful in correcting vicious habits of pronunciation and in strengthening the vocal organs.

As a rule, only one or two sounds should be employed at one lesson. Care should be taken that the pupils observe and practice these sounds correctly in their reading.

TABLE OF VOCALS.

LONG SOUNDS.

ā,	as in	āte.	ẽ,	as in	ẽrr.
â,	"	eâre.	ī,	"	īçe.
ä,	"	ärm.	ō,	"	ōde.
ȧ,	"	lȧst.	ū,	"	ūse.
a̤,	"	a̤ll.	û,	"	bûrn.
ē,	"	ēve.	o͞o,	"	fo͞ol.

SHORT SOUNDS.

ă, as in ăm.	ŏ, as in ŏdd.
ĕ, " ĕlm.	ŭ, " ŭp.
ĭ, " ĭn.	o͝o, " lo͝ok.

DIPHTHONGS.

oi, as in oil.	ou, as in out.

TABLE OF SUBVOCALS.

b, as in bĭb.	v, as in vălve.
d, " dĭd.	th, " thĭs.
g, " ḡĭḡ.	z, " zĭne.
j, " jŭḡ.	z, " ăzure.
n, " nīne.	r, " râre.
m, " māim.	w, " wē.
ng, " hăng.	y, " yĕt.

l, as in lŭll.

TABLE OF ASPIRATES.

f, as in fīfe.	t, as in tärt.
h, " hĭm.	sh, " shē.
k, " eāke.	ch, " chăt.
p, " pīpe.	th, " thĭck.
s, " sāme.	wh, " whȳ.

TABLE OF SUBSTITUTES.

ạ,	for ŏ,	as in	whạt.
ê,	" â,	"	thêre.
ẹ,	" ā,	"	fẹint.
ï,	" ē,	"	poliçe.
ῑ,	" ẽ,	"	sῑr.
ȯ,	" ŭ,	"	sȯn.
ọ,	" o͞o,	"	tọ.
ọ,	" o͝o,	"	wọlf.
ô,	" ạ,	"	fôrk.
õ,	" û,	"	wõrk.
ụ,	" o͝o,	"	fụll.
u̱,	" o͞o,	"	ru̱de
ȳ,	" ῑ.	"	flȳ.

y̆,	for ῑ,	as in	my̆th.
e,	" k,	"	ean.
ç,	" s,	"	çīte.
çh,	" sh,	"	çhāiṣe.
eh,	" k,	"	ehāos.
ġ,	" j,	"	ġĕm.
n̠,	" ng,	"	ïn̠k.
ṣ,	" z,	"	ăṣ.
s,	" sh,	"	su̱re.
x̱,	" g̱z,	"	ĕx̱ăet.
gh,	" f,	"	läugh.
ph,	" f,	"	phlŏx.
qu,	" k,	"	pïque.

qu, for kw, as in quĭt.

PUNCTUATION.

Punctuation Marks are used to make the sense more clear.

A **Period** (.) is used at the end of a sentence, and after an abbreviation; as,

James was quite sick. Dr. Jones was called to see him.

An Interrogation Mark (?) is used at the end of a question; as,

Where is John going?

An Exclamation Mark (!) is used after words or sentences expressing some strong feeling; as,

Alas, my noble boy! that thou shouldst die!

The Comma (,), Semicolon (;), and Colon (:) are used to separate the parts of a sentence.

The Hyphen (-) is used to join the parts of a compound word; as, *text-book:* it is also used at the end of a line in print or script, when a word is divided; as in the word *"sentence,"* near the bottom of page 9.

SECOND READER.

LESSON I.

newş'pā per	eōld	ôr'der	sēem	throügh
stŏck'ingş	chăt	stō'ry	light	Hăr'ry
brånch'eş	kĭss	bûrnş	Mrs.	e vĕnts'
an óth'er	Mr.	stōōl	lămp	mĕndş

EVENING AT HOME.

1. It is winter. The cold wind whis-
tles through the branches of the trees.

2. Mr. Brown has done his day's work, and his children, Harry and Kate, have come home from school. They learned their lessons well to-day, and both feel happy

3. Tea is over. Mrs. Brown has put the little sitting room in order. The fire burns brightly. One lamp gives light enough for all. On the stool is a basket of fine apples. They seem to say, "Won't you have one?"

4. Harry and Kate read a story in a new book. The father reads his newspaper, and the mother mends Harry's stockings.

5. By and by, they will tell one another what they have been reading about, and will have a chat over the events of the day.

6. Harry and Kate's bedtime will come first. I think I see them kiss their dear father and mother a sweet good night.

7. Do you not wish that every boy and girl could have a home like this?

LESSON II.

beaū'ti fụl   pōrch

rāin'bōw   bûrst

bŭb'bleş   sāme

bĭḡ'ḡest

snēeze

eȯl'orş

mīne   sōap   wạsh   rĕd   ma'ny (mĕn'y̆)

BUBBLES.

1. The boys have come out on the porch to blow bubbles. The old cat is asleep on the mat by the door.

2. "Ha! ha!" laughs Robert, as a bubble comes down softly on the old cat's back, and does not burst.

3. Willie tries to make his bubble do the same. This time it comes down on the cat's face, and makes her sneeze.

4. "She would rather wash her face without soap," says Harry. "Now let us see who can make the biggest bubble."

5. "Mine is the biggest," says Robert. "See how high it floats in the air! I can see—ah! it has burst."

6. "I can see the house and the trees and the sky in mine," says Willie; "and such beautiful colors."

7. "How many, Willie?"

8. "Red, one; blue, two; there—they are all out. Let us try again."

9. "I know how many colors there are," says Harry. "Just as many as there are in the rainbow."

10. "Do you know how many that is?"

LESSON III.

rŭb′ber	ḡŭn	pär′lor	strēet
nŭm′ber	tĕn	o′clŏck′	shōōt

WILLIE'S LETTER.

New York, Dec. 10, 1878.

Dear Santa Claus:

Papa is going to give me a Christmas tree, and he says that you will put nice things on it if I ask you. I would like a gun that will shoot, and a rubber ball that I can throw hard, and that will not break Mamma's windows or the big glass in the parlor.

Now, please don't forget to come. I live on Fourth St., number ten.

I will go to bed at eight o'clock, and shut my eyes tight.

I will not look indeed I won't.

Your little boy
Willie.

LESSON IV.

a bȯve′　　world　　därk　　ŏft
něv′er　　spärk　　dew　　tĭll
dī′a mond　　twĭn′kle　　blāz′ing

THE LITTLE STAR.

1. Twinkle, twinkle, little star;
How I wonder what you are,
Up above the world so high,
Like a diamond in the sky!

2. When the blazing sun is set,
And the grass with dew is wet,
Then you show your little light;
Twinkle, twinkle, all the night.

3. Then, if I were in the dark,
I would thank you for your spark.
I could not see which way to go,
If you did not twinkle so.

4. And when I am sound asleep,
Oft you through my window peep;
For you never shut your eye,
Till the sun is in the sky.

LESSON V.

be hīnd'	to ḡĕth'er	nō'ble	Sĕŏtch
Dŏdḡ'er	mĭn'utes	erĭb	wăḡ'on
tĕr'ri er	eoŭn'try	seōld	fĕl'low
shăḡ'ḡy	frĭsk'i ly	fīts	çĕl'lar
ḡuärdṣ	New'foŭnd land	yärd	här'ness

TWO DOGS.

1. James White has two dogs. One is a Newfoundland dog, and the other is a Scotch terrier.

2. The Newfoundland is a large, noble

2, 2.

fellow. He is black, with a white spot, and with long, shaggy hair. His name is Sport.

3. Sport is a good watchdog, and a kind playfellow. Every night he guards the house while James and his father are asleep.

4. In the daytime, James often uses Sport for his horse. He has a little wagon, and a set of small harness which just fits the dog.

5. He hitches Sport to this wagon, and drives over the country. In this way, he can go almost as fast as his father with the old family horse.

6. The name of James's Scotch terrier is Dodger. He is called Dodger because he jumps about so friskily. He is up on a chair, under the table, behind the door, down cellar, and out in the yard,—all in a minute.

7. Dodger has very bright eyes, and he does many funny things. He likes to put his paws up on the crib, and watch the baby.

8. The other day he took baby's **red** stocking, and had great fun with it; but he spoiled it in his play, and James had to scold him.

9. Every one likes to see James White with his two dogs. They always seem very happy together.

LESSON VI.

be twēen'	bū'reau (-ro)	stâirṣ	nēe'dle
a frāid'	shăd'ow	hĕld	stīr

AFRAID IN THE DARK.

1. "Willie, will you run upstairs, and get my needlebook from the bureau?"

2. But Willie did not stir. "Willie!" said mamma. She thought he had not heard.

3. "I'm afraid," said Willie.

4. "Afraid of what?"

5. "It's dark up there."

6. "What is the dark?" asked mamma. "See! It is nothing but a shadow."

And she held her hand between the lamp and the workbasket on the table.

7. "Now it is dark in the basket; but as soon as I take my hand away, it is light."

8. "Come and stand between the lamp and the wall, Willie. See! There is your shadow on the wall. Can your shadow hurt you?"

9. "Oh no, mamma! I am sure it can not hurt me."

10. "Well, the dark is only a big shadow over everything."

11. "What makes the big shadow, mamma?"

12. "I will tell you all about that, Willie, when you are a little older. But now, I wish you would find me a brave boy who is not afraid of shadows, to run upstairs and get my needlebook."

13. "I am brave, mamma. I will go. —Here it is."

14. "Thank you, my brave little man. You see the dark did n't hurt you."

SLATE. WORK.

Beautiful faces are they that wear
The light of a pleasant spirit there;
Beautiful hands are they that do
Deeds that are noble good and true;
Beautiful feet are they that go
Swiftly to lighten another's woe.

LESSON VII.

spĭ′ derṣ

stāy

nōṣe

erạwlṣ

bĕck

ḡōeṣ

spĕck

dŏt

shọeṣ   sprĕad   be liĕve′

tĭck′ling

nĕck

sē′eret

lĕḡṣ

ōpe

tōeṣ

chōōṣe

nŏd

sĭx

BABY BYE.

1.   Baby Bye,
    Here 's a fly;
    We will watch him, you and I.
      How he crawls
      Up the walls,
      Yet he never falls!
    I believe with six such legs
    You and I could walk on eggs.
      There he goes
      On his toes,
      Tickling Baby's nose.

2. Spots of red
   Dot his head;
   Rainbows on his back are spread;
    That small speck
    Is his neck;
    See him nod and beck!
   I can show you, if you choose,
   Where to look to find his shoes,
    Three small pairs,
    Made of hairs;
    These he always wears.

3. Flies can see
   More than we;
   So how bright their eyes must be!
    Little fly,
    Ope your eye;
    Spiders are near by.
   For a secret I can tell,
   Spiders never use flies well;
    Then away,
    Do not stay.
    Little fly, good day.

LESSON VIII.

sẽrv'ant   sŭd'den ly

lŏn͟'ger   re tûrned'

lived   tīred

sinçe   fīve

ă͟nx'iŏŭs

troŭ'ble

çēr'tain

nēar'ly

dŏz'en

sĕv'en

ăt'tic   strănġe

ḡreāt   prŏp'er

cōal   sēemed

PUSS AND HER KITTENS.

1. Puss, with her three kittens, had lived in the coal cellar; but one day she thought she would carry them to the attic.

2. The servant thought that was

not the proper place for them; so she carried them back to the cellar.

3. Puss was certain that she wanted them in the attic; so she carried them there again and again, five, six, seven, —yes, a dozen times; for each time the servant took them back to the cellar.

4. Poor puss was nearly tired out, and could carry them no longer.

5. Suddenly she went away. Where do you think she went?

6. She was gone a long time. When she returned, she had a strange cat with her that we had never seen before.

7. She seemed to tell him all about her great trouble, and he listened to her story.

8. Then the strange cat took the little kittens, one by one, and carried them to the attic. After this he went away, and we have never seen him since.

9. The servant then left the kittens in the attic, for she saw how anxious puss was to have them stay there.

10. Was not the strange cat kind to puss? This lesson should teach children to be ever ready to help one another.

LESSON IX.

nine   mous′ie

frō   frŏl′ie

bĭt   slĭpped

spīed

erōw

tēeth

pẽarl

ūẓed

KITTY AND MOUSIE.

1. Once there was a little kitty,
    White as the snow;
In a barn he used to frolic,
    Long time ago.

2. In the barn a little mousie
    Ran to and fro;
For she heard the little kitty,
    Long time ago.

3. Two black eyes had little kitty,
    Black as a crow;
And they spied the little mousie,
    Long time ago.

4. Four soft paws had little kitty,
    Paws soft as snow;
And they caught the little mousie,
    Long time ago.

5. Nine pearl teeth had little kitty,
    All in a row;
And they bit the little mousie,
    Long time ago.

6. When the teeth bit little mousie,
    Mousie cried out "Oh!"
But she slipped away from kitty,
    Long time ago.

LESSON X.

wạshed	hourṣ (ourṣ)	prĕ′cioŭs	ğāme
härm	a̤′ny (ĕn′y̆)	brŭshed	ĕnd

AT WORK.

1. A little play does not harm any one, but does much good. After play, we should be glad to work.

2. I knew a boy who liked a good game very much. He could run, swim, jump, and play ball; and was always merry when out of school.

3. But he knew that time is not all for play; that our minutes, hours, and days are very precious.

4. At the end of his play, he would go home. After he had washed his face and hands, and brushed his hair, he would help his mother, or read in his book, or write upon his slate.

5. He used to say, "One thing at a time." When he had done with work, he would play; but he did not try to play and to work at the same time.

LESSON XI.

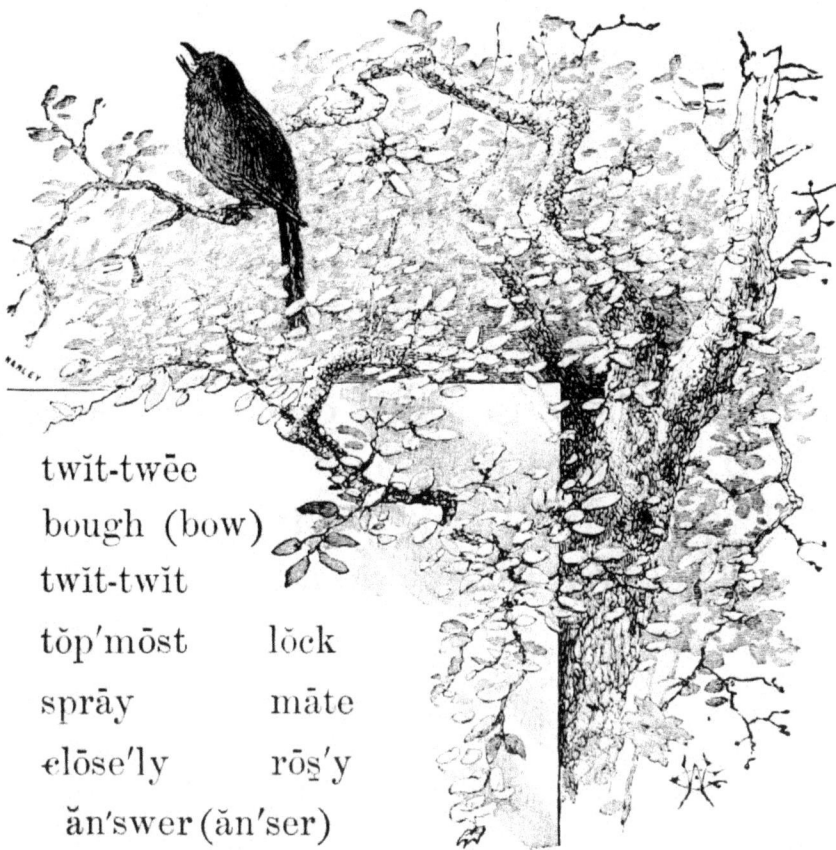

twĭt-twēe
bough (bow)
twĭt-twĭt
tŏp'mōst   lŏck
sprāy   māte
elōse'ly   rōṣ'y
ăn'swer (ăn'ser)

WHAT A BIRD TAUGHT.

1. Why do you come to my apple tree,
    Little bird so gray?
  Twit-twit, twit-twit, twit-twit-twee!
    That was all he would say.

2. Why do you lock your rosy feet
   So closely round the spray?
   Twit-twit, twit-twit, twit-tweet!
   That was all he would say.

3. Why on the topmost bough do you get,
   Little bird so gray?
   Twit-twit-twee! twit-twit-twit!
   That was all he would say.

4. Where is your mate? come, answer me,
   Little bird so gray.
   Twit-twit-twit! twit-twit-twee!
   That was all he would say.

Alice Cary.

LESSON XII.

brīght'ness	plĕaṣ'ant	lēarned	drĕss
plāy'mātes	ŭn kīnd'	răḡ'ḡed	wôrd
quĕs'tionṣ	smīl'ing	erōwed	chīld
Sŭn'bēam	chēered	Sū'ṣie	ḡāve
ḡlăd'ness	un lĕss'	nāme	ḡāte

SUSIE SUNBEAM.

1. Susie Sunbeam was not her real name; that was Susan Brown. But every

one called her Susie Sunbeam, because she had such a sweet, smiling face, and always brought brightness with her when she came.

2. Her grandfather first gave her this name, and it seemed to fit the little girl so nicely that soon it took the place of her own.

3. Even when a baby, Susie laughed and crowed from morning till night. No one ever heard her cry unless she was sick or hurt.

4. When she had learned to walk,

she loved to go about the house and get things for her mother, and in this way save her as many steps as she could.

5. She would sit by her mother's side for an hour at a time, and ask her ever so many questions, or she would take her new book and read.

6. Susie was always pleasant in her play with other children. She never used an unkind word, but tried to do whatever would please her playmates best.

7. One day, a poor little girl with a very ragged dress was going by, and Susie heard some children teasing her and making fun of her.

8. She at once ran out to the gate, and asked the poor little girl to come in. "What are you crying for?" Susie asked.

9. "Because they all laugh at me," she said.

10. Then Susie took the little girl into the house. She cheered her up with

kind words, and gave her a nice dress and a pair of shoes.

11. This brought real joy and gladness to the poor child, and she, too, thought that Susie was rightly called Sunbeam.

LESSON XIII.

wŏŏd'lăndṣ	dĭ vīne'	rāiṣed	un tĭl'
drōōp'ing	blĕssed	whoṣe	sēek
ŭp'ward	hŏv'elṣ	ĭn'ner	stēal
hĕav'en	heärts	lĭl'ieṣ	dīe
	rōam'ing		

IF I WERE A SUNBEAM.

1. "If I were a sunbeam,
　　I know what I'd do;
　I would seek white lilies,
　　Roaming woodlands through.
　I would steal among them,
　　Softest light I'd shed,
　Until every lily
　　Raised its drooping head.
2, 3.

2. "If I were a sunbeam,
　　　I know where I'd go;
　Into lowly hovels,
　　　Dark with want and woe:
　Till sad hearts looked upward,
　　　I would shine and shine;
　Then they'd think of heaven,
　　　Their sweet home and mine."

3. Are you not a sunbeam,
　　　Child, whose life is glad
　With an inner brightness
　　　Sunshine never had?
　Oh, as God has blessed you,
　　　Scatter light divine!
　For there is no sunbeam
　　　But must die or shine.

LESSON XIV.

sup pōrt'   a lŏng'   bōōts

be lŏng'   dŏl'lar   yēarṣ

măn'aġe

taught

eôr'ner

nō'tĭçe

mȯn'ey

blăck'ing

ġĕn'tle men

hŏn'est (ŏn'est)   quīte   buȳ   ẽarned

HENRY, THE BOOTBLACK.

1. Henry was a kind, good boy. His father was dead, and his mother was very poor. He had a little sister about two years old.

2. He wanted to help his mother, for she could not always earn enough to buy food for her little family.

3. One day, a man gave him a dollar for finding a pocketbook which he had lost.

4. Henry might have kept all the money, for no one saw him when he found it. But his mother had taught him to be honest, and never to keep what did not belong to him.

5. With the dollar he bought a box, three brushes, and some blacking. He then went to the corner of the street, and said to every one whose boots did not look nice, "Black your boots, sir, please?"

6. He was so polite that gentlemen soon began to notice him, and to let him black their boots. The first day he brought home fifty cents, which he gave to his mother to buy food with.

7. When he gave her the money, she said, as she dropped a tear of joy, "You are a dear, good boy, Henry. I did not know how I could earn enough to buy bread with, but now I think we can manage to get along quite well."

8. Henry worked all the day, and went to school in the evening. He earned almost enough to support his mother and his little sister.

LESSON XV.

trĕad	whĭs'per	sŏft'ly
talk	chēer ful	eâre'ful

DON'T WAKE THE BABY.

Baby sleeps, so we must tread
Softly round her little bed,
And be careful that our toys
Do not fall and make a noise.

We must not talk, but whisper low,
Mother wants to work, we know,
That, when father comes to tea,
All may neat and cheerful be.

LESSON XVI.

full	lõad	hĕav′y	mĭd′dle	hĕav′i er
slĭp	wrŏng	hăn′dle	brŏth′er	de çēived′

A KIND BROTHER.

1. A boy was once sent from home to take a basket of things to his grandmother.

2. The basket was so full that it was very heavy. So his little brother went with him, to help carry the load.

3. They put a pole under the handle of the basket, and each then took hold of an end of the pole. In this way they could carry the basket very nicely.

4. Now the older boy thought, "My brother Tom does not know about this pole.

5. "If I slip the basket near him, his side will be heavy, and mine light; but if the basket is in the middle of the pole, it will be as heavy for me as it is for him.

6. "Tom does not know this as I do. But I will not do it. It would be wrong, and I will not do what is wrong."

7. Then he slipped the basket quite near his own end of the pole. His load was now heavier than that of his little brother.

8. Yet he was happy; for he felt that he had done right. Had he deceived his brother, he would not have felt at all happy.

LESSON XVII.

buṣ'y (bĭz'zy)	mĭs'chĭef	lŏŏked	ŭn'tọ	ḡlēe
ҫon trīv'ing	rĭng'lets	nŏd'dle	drew	nŭn
prĕss'ing	fĭṉ'ḡerṣ	ҫär'pet	wīṣe	lĭps
em brāҫe'	pŏn'der	lăsh'eṣ	ҫlīmb	trụe

MY GOOD-FOR-NOTHING.

1. "What are you good for, my brave little
man?
Answer that question for me, if you can,—
You, with your fingers as white as a nun,—
You, with your ringlets as bright as the sun.
All the day long, with your busy contriving,
Into all mischief and fun you are driving;
See if your wise little noddle can tell
What you are good for. Now ponder it well."

2. Over the carpet the dear little feet
Came with a patter to climb on my seat;
Two merry eyes, full of frolic and glee,
Under their lashes looked up unto me;
Two little hands pressing soft on my face,
Drew me down close in a loving embrace;
Two rosy lips gave the answer so true,
"Good to love you, mamma, good to love you."

Emily Huntington Miller.

LESSON XVIII.

bĕr′rieṣ

rŏb′in

shôrt

rĭd

därt

shärp

wŏrmṣ

strīkes

ēa′ḡle

kĭng

fōe

fāilṣ

hạwk

ăc′tĭve

THE KINGBIRD.

1. The kingbird is not bigger than a robin.

2. He eats flies, and worms, and bugs, and berries.

3. He builds his nest in a tree, near some house.

4. When there are young ones in the nest, he sits on the top of a tree near them.

5. He watches to see that no bird comes to hurt them or their mother.

6. If a hawk, a crow, or even an eagle comes near, he makes a dash at it.

7. Though he is so small, he is brave, and he is also very active.

8. He never fails to drive off other birds from his nest.

9. He flies around and around the eagle, and suddenly strikes him with his sharp bill.

10. He strikes at his eye, and then darts away before the eagle can catch him.

11. Or he strikes from behind, and is off again before the eagle can turn round.

12. In a short time, the great eagle is tired of such hard blows, and flies away. He is very glad to get rid of his foe.

13. Is not the little fellow a brave bird?

14. Because he can drive off all other birds, he is called the KINGBIRD.

LESSON XIX.

wạtch'ing	ğăth'erṣ	ān'ġelṣ	be ğĭn'
därk'ness	a ĕrŏss'	lōne'ly	bēasts

EVENING HYMN.

1. Now the day is over,
    Night is drawing nigh,
Shadows of the evening
    Steal across the sky.

2. Now the darkness gathers,
　　Stars begin to peep;
　Birds, and beasts, and flowers
　　Soon will be asleep.

3. Through the lonely darkness,
　　May the angels spread
　Their white wings above me,
　　Watching round my bed.

LESSON XX.

dĭ vīd'ed	quạr'rel	a ğrēe'	thŭs	sĕt'tle
sĕt'tling	kēr'nel	ē'qual	ăpt	pärts

THE QUARREL.

1. Under a great tree in the woods, two boys saw a fine, large nut, and both ran to get it.

2. James got to it first, and picked it up.

3. "It is mine," said John, "for I was the first to see it."

4. "No, it is mine," said James, "for I was the first to pick it up."

5. Thus, they at once began to quarrel about the nut.

6. As they could not agree whose it should be, they called an older boy, and asked him.

7. The older boy said, "I will settle this quarrel."

8. He took the nut, and broke the shell. He then took out the kernel,

and divided the shell into two parts, as nearly equal as he could.

9. "This half of the shell," said he, "belongs to the boy who first saw the nut.

10. "And this half belongs to the boy who picked it up.

11. "The kernel of the nut, I shall keep as my pay for settling the quarrel.

12. "This is the way," said he, laughing, "in which quarrels are very apt to end."

LESSON XXI.

crea'tūreş	drōneş	in'sīde	hīve	i'dle
de fĕnse'	drĭv'en	kĭlled	çĕllş	sīze
wõrk'erş	quēen	stĭngş	shāpe	wăx

THE BEE.

1. Bees live in a house that is called a hive. They are of three kinds,—workers, drones, and queens.

2. Only one queen can live in each hive. If she is lost or dead, the other bees will stop their work.

3. They are very wise and busy little creatures. They all join together to build cells of wax for their honey.

4. Each bee takes its proper place, and does its own work. Some go out and gather honey from the flowers; others stay at home and work inside the hive.

5. The cells which they build, are all of one shape and size, and no room is left between them.

6. The cells are not round, but have six sides.

7. Did you ever look into a glass hive to see the bees while at work? It is pleasant to see how busy they always are.

8. But the drones do not work. Before winter comes, all the drones are driven from the hive or killed, that they may not eat the honey which they did not gather.

9. It is not quite safe for children to handle bees. They have sharp stings that they know well how to use in their defense.

SLATE WORK.

How doth the little busy bee
Improve each shining hour,
And gather honey all the day
From every opening flower!

LESSON XXII.

blŏs′somş	drēar′y	wēa′ry	pĭnks
smĕll′ing	toil′ing	lĕv′ieş	bŭzz
frā′ḡrant	thĭs′tle	wēedş	sçĕnt
trĕaş′ūre	yĕl′lōw	mĕad′ow	tăx
sŭm′mer	ċlō′ver	ċloud′y	dāi′şy

dăf′fo dĭl lieş   ċŏl′um bīne   hŭm′ming

THE SONG OF THE BEE.

1. Buzz! buzz! buzz!
    This is the song of the bee.
    His legs are of yellow;
    A jolly, good fellow,
        And yet a great worker is he.
2, 4.

2. In days that are sunny
   He's getting his honey;
   In days that are cloudy
      He's making his wax:
   On pinks and on lilies,
   And gay daffodillies,
   And columbine blossoms,
      He levies a tax!

3. Buzz! buzz! buzz!
   The sweet-smelling clover,
   He, humming, hangs over;
   The scent of the roses
      Makes fragrant his wings:
   He never gets lazy;
   From thistle and daisy,
   And weeds of the meadow,
      Some treasure he brings.

4. Buzz! buzz! buzz!
   From morning's first light
   Till the coming of night,
   He's singing and toiling
      The summer day through.

Oh! we may get weary,
And think work is dreary;
'Tis harder by far
To have nothing to do.

Marian Douglas.

LESSON XXIII.

un hăp′py
hēed′less
grōw′ing
härsh′ly
ĕaṣ′i ly

prŏm′īsed
be căme′
eâre′less
lēav′ing
ef fĕets′

| an noy′ | mä'am | blāme | wŏrse | tŏrn |
| härd′ly | nīç′est | spĕnd | hăb′it | ē′vil |

THE TORN DOLL.

1. Mary Armstrong was a pretty little girl, but she was heedless about some things.

2. Her way of leaving her books and playthings just where she had used them last, gave her mother much trouble in picking them up and putting them in their proper places.

3. She had often told Mary the evil effects of being so careless. Her books became spoiled, and her toys broken.

4. But worse than this was the growing habit of carelessness, which would be of great harm to her all her life. It would make her unhappy, and would annoy her friends.

5. One day Mary and her mother went out into their pleasant yard, to spend an hour in the open air. Mrs. Armstrong took her work with her.

6. Mary ran about and played with Dash, her pet dog, and was having a happy time.

7. But in a corner of the yard she found her nicest doll all torn and broken, and its dress covered with mud.

8. She knew, at once, that Dash had done this, and she scolded him harshly.

9. Carrying the broken doll to her mamma, she showed it to her, and could hardly keep from crying.

10. Mrs. Armstrong asked Mary if she had not left the doll on the porch where Dash could easily get it; and Mary had to answer, "Yes, ma'am."

11. "Then you must not blame the dog, Mary, for he does not know it is wrong for him to play with your doll. I hope this will be a lesson to you hereafter, to put your things away when you are through playing."

12. "I will try," said Mary. And her mother promised to mend the doll as well as she could.

LESSON XXIV.

thŏr′ōugh ly	mŏnth	drīed	dȳed	eŭts
shēar′er	shēep	thōṣe	spŭn	dīrt
ŏth′er wiṣe	wōv′en	elŏth	wŏol	rŭb

SHEEP-SHEARING.

1. Sheep are washed and sheared some time in the month of June. This should be done quite early in the month, before the hot days begin.

2. It is fine sport for those who look on, but not much fun for the sheep.

3. It is best for the sheep to have the wool taken off; otherwise they would suffer in the summer time.

4. When the time comes for washing the sheep, they are driven to a pond or a little river.

5. Then they are thrown into the water, one at a time. The men who are in the water catch them, and squeeze the wet wool with their hands to get the dirt all out of it.

6. When the wool is thoroughly dried, the sheep are taken to the shearer; and he cuts off the wool with a large pair of shears.

7. It is then dyed, spun, and woven into cloth.

8. In a short time, before the cold winter comes, new wool grows out on the sheep. By the coming of spring there is so much, that it must be cut off again.

beâr′erş	ēarth	wạrm	sŭl′try
wạn′der	rāyş	ḡrāin	eloudş
	ō′er	wē′re	

THE CLOUDS.

1.

"Clouds that wander through the sky,
Sometimes low and sometimes high;
In the darkness of the night,
In the sunshine warm and bright.
Ah! I wonder much if you
Have any useful work to do."

2.

"Yes, we're busy night and day,
As o'er the earth we take our way.
We are bearers of the rain
To the grass, and flowers, and grain;
We guard you from the sun's bright rays,
In the sultry summer days."

LESSON XXVI.

pēo'ple   fŏr'est

squir'rel   eōōl

nēar'est   tāme

hŏl'low   snŭḡ

shōul'der   mileş

stĭcks

ġĕn'tle

thōugh

Păt'ty

PATTY AND THE SQUIRREL.

1. Little Patty lives in a log house near a great forest. She has no sisters, and her big brothers are away all day helping their father.

2. But Patty is never lonely; for, though the nearest house is miles away,

she has many little friends. Here are two of them that live in the woods.

3. But how did Patty teach them to be so tame? Patty came to the woods often, and was always so quiet and gentle that the squirrels soon found they need not be afraid of her.

4. She brought her bread and milk to eat under the trees, and was sure to leave crumbs for the squirrels.

5. When they came near, she sat very still and watched them. So, little by little, she made them her friends, till, at last, they would sit on her shoulder, and eat from her hand.

6. Squirrels build for themselves summer houses. These are made of leaves, and sticks, and moss. They are nice and cool for summer, but would never do for the winter cold and snow.

7. So these wise little people find a hollow in an old tree. They make it warm and snug with soft moss and leaves; and here the squirrels live all through the long winter.

LESSON XXVII.

frīght′ened	in tĕnd′	whēat	Thŏm′as
ꞓom plāinş′	plŭmş	chōōşe	shŏck′ing
spăr′row	rīp′est	rŏb′bing	brĕak′fast

plĕn′ty   shâre   trēat   tāleş   wāit

THE SPARROW.

1. Glad to see you, little bird;
   'Twas your little chirp I heard:
   What did you intend to say?
   "Give me something this cold day"?

2. That I will, and plenty, too;
   All the crumbs I saved for you.
   Do n't be frightened—here's a treat:
   I will wait and see you eat.

3. Shocking tales I hear of you;
   Chirp, and tell me, are they true?
   Robbing all the summer long;
   Do n't you think it very wrong?

4. Thomas says you steal his wheat;
   John complains, his plums you eat—
   Choose the ripest for your share,
   Never asking whose they are.

5. But I will not try to know
   What you did so long ago:
   There's your breakfast, eat away;
   Come to see me every day.

LESSON XXVIII.

äft'er nōon
sŭp'per
dēep
lĕngth
ear'rïaġe
threw

hĕdġe stŏŏd tru̸'ly rōad few săd

SAM AND HARRY.

1. One fine summer afternoon, Sam was walking home from school. He went along slowly, reading a book.

2. Sam had spent all his money for the book, but he was a happy boy.

3. At length he came into the high-road, where there was a gate. A blind man stood, holding it open.

4. The poor man said, "Please give me a few cents to buy some bread!" But Sam gave him nothing.

5. What! did Sam give the poor blind man nothing? Yes; for, as I told you, he had spent all his money.

6. So Sam walked on, very sad. Soon after, a fine carriage came up, and in it were Harry and his mother.

7. The blind man stood, and held out his hat. "Let us give the poor man something," said Harry to his mother.

8. His mother gave him some cents. Harry took them, but did not put them into the man's hat.

9. He threw them into the hedge as far as he could. The poor man could not find them, for, you know, he was blind.

10. Sam had turned back to look at the fine carriage. He saw Harry throw

the cents into the hedge; so he came back at once, and looked for the money until he found it all for the blind man.

11. This took so long a time, that he almost lost his supper.

12. Which of the boys do you think was truly kind to the poor man?

13. I know which he thanked most in his heart.

LESSON XXIX.

rĭp′pling	frĭnġe	strāy	thou	mĭll
vĭl′laġe	brĭnk	clēar	wīld	hĭll
cōurse	bāthe	tī′ny	pōōl	rĭll

THE LITTLE RILL.

1. Run, run, thou tiny rill;
   Run, and turn the village mill;
   Run, and fill the deep, clear pool
   In the woodland's shade so cool,
   Where the sheep love best to stray
   In the sultry summer day;
   Where the wild birds bathe and drink,
   And the wild flowers fringe the brink.

2. Run, run, thou tiny rill,
Round the rocks, and down
the hill;
Sing to every child like me;
The birds will join you, full
of glee:
And we will listen to the
song
You sing, your rip-
pling course along.

hās'tened	pŏs'si ble	băl'ançe	Ed'ḡar	sǎve
boat'man	dān'ḡer	quĭck'ly	mọve	trĭp
strĕtched	sĕv'er al	stärt'ed	fōlks	fĕll

THE BOAT UPSET.

1. "Sit still, children. Do not move about in the boat," said Mr. Rose to the young folks he was taking for a trip on the water.

2. The boat was a large one, and could not easily be upset. There were in it Mr. and Mrs. Rose, the boatman, and several little boys and girls.

3. "Keep still, please, young gentlemen," said the boatman, when Edgar Rose and Thomas Read began to move from one side to the other.

4. They kept quiet for a short time only. Edgar soon wanted a stick which Thomas held in his hand. He lost his balance in trying to get the stick, and fell into the water.

2, 5.

5. Mr. and Mrs. Rose both started up, and stretched out their arms to save him; but in so doing, they upset the boat.

6. Every one fell into the water, and all were in the greatest danger of being drowned.

7. Another boat was near, with but one man in it. He hastened to them as quickly as possible, and saved them from drowning.

8. Children should always be careful and quiet when they are in a boat on the water, and should obey what older people tell them.

LESSON XXXI.

MARY'S LETTER.

Forest Hill, June 25, 1878.
My Dear Fanny:
This morning, while out rowing, we all came near being drowned. Brother Ed, in trying to take a stick from Tom Reed, tripped and fell out of the boat. Papa and Mamma caught at him to save him, and before we knew it we were all in the water. The boat upset and how we were all saved I can hardly tell. A man in another boat which was near, picked us up.

Had it not been for this, you would to-day have no cousin.
Mary Rose.

LESSON XXXII.

lĭ'on	bŏd'y	strīpes	de līght'	Eng'lish
prey	tī'ger	eŏl'lar	tī'gress	frīght'fụl
sēize	chāin	un līke'	swĭft'est	ăn'i malṣ
rōar	ġī'ant	slīght'est	ŏf'fi çerṣ	whĭsk'erṣ

THE TIGER.

1. The tiger is a giant cat. His body is nearly covered with black stripes.

2. Unlike the lion, he runs so fast that the swiftest horse can not over-take him. He goes over the ground by

making bounds or springs, one after another.

3. By night, as well as by day, the tiger watches for his prey. With a frightful roar, he will seize a man, and carry him off.

4. Have you ever thought what use whiskers are to cats? Lions have great whiskers, and so have tigers and all other animals of the cat kind.

5. Whenever you find an animal with whiskers like the cat's, you may be sure that animal steals softly among branches and thick bushes.

6. By the slightest touch on the tiger's whiskers, he knows when there is anything in his road.

7. A few years ago, some English officers went out to hunt. When coming home from their day's sport, they found a little tiger kitten.

8. They took it with them and tied it, with a collar and chain, to the pole of their tent. It played about, to the delight of all who saw it.

9. One evening, just as it was growing dark, they heard a sound that frightened them greatly. It was the roar of a tiger.

10. The kitten pulled at the chain, and tried to break away. With a sharp cry, it answered the voice outside.

11. All at once, a large tigress bounded into the middle of the tent. She caught her kitten by the neck, and broke the chain which bound it.

12. Then turning to the door of the tent, she dashed away as suddenly as she had come.

LESSON XXXIII.

thĕn	ū'ṣu al	eoŭṣ'in	fīre'sīde	sew'ing (sō-)
Kā'tie	bĕt'ter	erăc'kle	knĭt'ting	per hăps'
Jāne	rēa'ṣon	to-nīght'	hăp'pi er	in strŭet'ĭve

THE FIRESIDE.

1. One winter night, Mrs. Lord and her two little girls sat by a bright fire

in their pleasant home. The girls were sewing, and their mother was busy at her knitting.

2. At last, Katie finished her work, and, looking up, said, "Mother, I think the fire is brighter than usual. How I love to hear it crackle!"

3. "And I was about to say," cried Mary, "that this is a better light than we had last night."

4. "My dears," said their mother, "it

must be that you feel happier than usual to-night. Perhaps that is the reason why you think the fire better, and the light brighter."

5. "But, mother," said Mary, "I do not see why we are happier now than we were then; for last night cousin Jane was here, and we played 'Puss in the corner' and 'Blind man' until we all were tired."

6. "I know! I know why!" said Katie. "It is because we have all been doing something useful to-night. We feel happy because we have been busy."

7. "You are right, my dear," said their mother. "I am glad you have both learned that there may be something more pleasant than play, and, at the same time, more instructive."

LESSON XXXIV.

dew'drops	hŏp'ping	lā'zi est	bĕndṣ	sŭng
pā'tiençe	in stĕad'	där'ling	ôught	rĕst
slŭm'ber	my sĕlf'	re plȳ'	mĭss	loṣe

BIRDIE'S MORNING SONG.

1. Wake up, little darling, the birdies are out,
   And here you are still in your nest!
The laziest birdie is hopping about;
   You ought to be up with the rest.
Wake up, little darling, wake up!

2. Oh, see what you miss when you slumber
      so long—
   The dewdrops, the beautiful sky!
I can not sing half what you lose in my song;
   And yet, not a word in reply.
Wake up, little darling, wake up!

3. I've sung myself quite out of patience with
    you,
While mother bends o'er your dear head;
Now birdie has, done all that birdie can do:
    Her kisses will wake you instead!
Wake up, little darling, wake up!

George Cooper.

LESSON XXXV.

sĕnt	stōre	Bounçe	flōat'ing
loud	çĭr'ele	rĭp'pleṣ	eătch'ing
eāke	blŏcks	strōlled	how ĕv'er

WILLIE AND BOUNCE.

1. Two fast friends were Willie Brown and his little dog Bounce. Willie could never think of taking a walk without Bounce. Cake and play were equally shared between them.

2. Willie taught his dog many cunning tricks, and often said that Bounce could do almost anything in the world but talk.

3. There came a time, however, when Bounce really told Willie's father some-

thing, though he could not talk. Let
me tell you how he did this.

4. It was on a bright summer afternoon. Willie had strolled with Bounce
down to the river, which was not more
than two blocks from his father's store.

5. Willie began to throw stones into
the water, and to watch the ripples as
they made one circle after another.

6. Bounce lay on the grass, watching the flies that buzzed around his nose, and catching any that came too near.

7. There were some logs floating in the river near the shore. Willie jumped upon one of them, to see if he could throw a stone across the river.

8. He drew back, and sent the stone with all his might. Just as it left his hand, the log turned, and he fell into the water.

9. He was very much frightened, for he did not know how to swim, and there was no one to hear, though he called as loud as he could for help.

LESSON XXXVI.

yĕlp	loud'ly	a ḡainst'	lŏŏk'ing	bärk'ing
sprăng	clōtheṣ	ō'pened	dis trĕss'	serătched

WILLIE AND BOUNCE.

(CONCLUDED.)

1. Poor little Bounce gave a great yelp of distress. If he had been a

big water dog, he could have jumped in and brought his master out.

2. He ran up and down the bank two or three times, barking, looking first at Willie and then around. Then he started, as fast as he could run, up the street to the store.

3. When he got there the door was shut, but he scratched against it and barked loudly, until some one came and opened it.

4. He caught hold of Mr. Brown's clothes, then ran to the door, then back again, catching at him, barking, and jumping.

5. A friend who was in the store said to Mr. Brown, "Something must be wrong; I would put on my hat, and go with the dog." Bounce, seeing Mr. Brown take his hat, started for the river.

6. Then Mr. Brown thought of Willie. As he came . to the river, he saw Willie's hat floating on the water, and his small arm thrown up.

7. He sprang in and caught him just as he was going down for the last time, and quickly carried him to the bank. Willie soon got over his fright, and no one seemed to be more delighted than Bounce.

LESSON XXXVII.

tạlk′a tĭve

im prọve′

o blī′ġing

wrĭt′ten

tĭck-tŏck

€lŏck

trụth′fụl

it sĕlf′

kĭtch′en

fēar

rēach′eṣ

mōst

THE KITCHEN CLOCK.

1. Listen to the kitchen clock!
    To itself it ever talks,
    From its place it never walks;
   "Tick-tock—tick-tock:"
    Tell me what it says.

2. "I'm a very patient clock,
     Never moved by hope or fear,
     Though I've stood for many a year;
  Tick-tock—tick-tock:"
     That is what it says.

3. "I'm a very truthful clock:
     People say about the place,
     Truth is written on my face;
  Tick-tock—tick-tock:"
     That is what it says.

4. "I'm a most obliging clock;
     If you wish to hear me strike,
     You may do it when you like;
  Tick-tock—tick-tock:"
     That is what it says.

5. "I'm a very friendly clock;
     For this truth to all I tell,
     Life is short, improve it well;
  Tick-tock—tick-tock:"
     That is what it says.

6. What a talkative old clock!
Let us see what it will do
When the hour hand reaches two;
"Ding-ding—tick-tock:"
That is what it says.

LESSON XXXVIII.

Hẽr'bert

fīnd

ĭnch'eṣ

bēam

pīne

ḡrōōve

hŏle

ḡĭm'let

ŏr'anġe

pōst

thrĕad

thĭck

nĕxt

seāleṣ

pēel

rĭb'bon

THE NEW SCALES.

1. "Herbert, will you please peel my orange?" said Lucy. Herbert was read-ing his new book, but he put it down

2. 6.

at once, and took the orange from his little sister.

2. "Shall I make a pair of scales, Lucy, for you to use when you play store?"

3. "Oh yes! but how can you do that?"

4. "I'll show you. First, we must take the peel off in two little cups, one just as large as the other. While I do this, see if you can find me two nice sticks about ten inches long."

5. Lucy ran out to the woodhouse to find the sticks.—"Will these do?"

6. "No, they are too hard. Find some pine sticks if you can."

7. "Here are some."

8. "These will do nicely. Now I must make a scalebeam and a post. Can you find me a little block for a post, Lucy?"

9. "Will a ribbon block do, Herbert?"

10. "Yes, if it is not too thick."

11. "Here is one an inch thick."

12. "That will be just right. Now get the little gimlet."

13. Herbert worked away until he had made the beam and the post. Then he made a hole in the middle of the block, and put the post in. Next, he put the beam into a little groove at the top of the post, so that it would balance nicely.

14. "Now, Lucy, we must have a needle and some thread. We must put four threads to each cup; then we will tie the threads to the ends of the beam.

15. "There, Lucy, what do you think of that?"

16. "Why, Herbert, that is just as nice as the real scales in father's store; and you may have all my orange for making them."

LESSON XXXIX.

smĕlt hīde
erĕpt lāid
flōor ĭnn
beâr fûr

yoŭng′est   dȧnçed   joy′fṳl ly   märched
sōl′dierṣ   băd′ly   rŭn′ning   ĕld′est

THE BEAR AND THE CHILDREN.

1. In the parlor of an inn in a small town, sat a man who had been

going about with a bear. He was waiting for his supper, and the bear was
tied up in the yard.

2. Up in the attic, three little children were playing together. The eldest
might have been six years old; the
youngest, not more than two.

3. Stump! stump! stump! Some one
was coming up the stairs.

4. The door flew open suddenly, and
there stood the great, shaggy bear. He
had got tired of waiting, and had found
his way to the stairs.

5. The children were badly frightened.
Each one crept into a corner, but the
bear found them all out, and smelt
their clothes, but did not hurt them.

6. "This must be a great dog," they
said, and they began to pat him.

7. Then the bear lay down on the
floor, and the youngest boy climbed on
his back, hid his head in the shaggy
fur, and played at "hide and seek."

8. The eldest boy took his drum and
began to strike it, when the bear rose

on his hind legs and danced. At that the children gave a merry shout.

9. The two younger boys took their wooden guns, and gave the bear one. Away they all marched around the room, keeping step.

10. Now the frightened mother of the children came to the door. But the youngest boy shouted, joyfully. "See, we are playing soldiers!"

11. Then the bear's master came running up, and took the bear away.

LESSON XL.

fâir	lā'dy	drēar	clĭng'ing	hâre'bĕll
flĕd	nê'er	de spâir'	nŏd'ding	blōōm'ing

THE LITTLE HAREBELL.

"Tell me, little harebell,
　　Are you lonely here,
Blooming in the shadow
　　On this rock so drear?"

Clinging to this bit of earth,
  As if in mid-air,
With your sweet face turned to me,
  Looking strangely fair?"

Lady" said the harebell,
  Nodding low its head,
Though this spot seems dreary,
  Though the sunlight's fled,

Know that I'm not lonely
  That I ne'er despair:
God is in the shadow
  God is everywhere".

LESSON XLI.

roŭgh (rŭf)

be nēath′

sēa′sīde

tĭm′id ly

rŏb′ber

spŏts

ŏs′prey

ŏf′ten (ŏf′n)

fiērçe′ly

twĕn′ty

eom pĕlş′

brĕast

mōde

hŏŏk′ed

THE FISHHAWK.

1. The fishhawk, or osprey, is not so large as the eagle; but he has, like the eagle, a hooked bill and sharp claws.

2. His color is a dark brown, with black and white spots, and his length is from twenty to twenty-two inches. His breast is mostly white. His tail and wings are long.

3. The fishhawk is often found sitting upon a tree over a pond, or lake,

or river. He is also found by the sea-side.

4. He watches the fish as they swim in the water beneath him; then he darts down suddenly and catches one of them.

5. When he catches a fish in his sharp, rough claws, he carries it off to eat, and, as he flies away with it for his dinner, an eagle sometimes meets him.

6. The eagle flies at him fiercely with his sharp bill and claws, and compels the hawk to drop the fish.

7. Then the eagle catches the fish as it falls, before it reaches the ground, and carries it off.

8. The poor fishhawk, with a loud cry, timidly flies away. He must go again to the water and catch another fish for his dinner.

9. Thus you see, that the eagle is a robber. He robs fishhawks, whose only mode of getting a living is by catching fish.

LESSON XLII.

lēaf	tȧsk	twīçe	sīgh'ing	hŏl'i dāyş
ḡāy	twĭḡ	mĕant	stŏpped	dĭf'fer ent
pŭff	ĕdġe	măt'ter	ạu'tumn	hŭn'dredş
lĕad	ḡrew	rŭs'tled	Oe tō'ber	trĕm'bling

WHAT THE LEAF SAID.

1. Once or twice a little leaf was
heard to cry and sigh, as leaves often

do when a gentle wind is blowing. And the twig said, "What is the matter, little leaf?"

2. "The wind," said the leaf, "just told me that one day it would pull me off, and throw me on the ground to die."

3. The twig told it to the branch, and the branch told it to the tree. When the tree heard it, it rustled all over, and sent word back to the trembling leaf.

4. "Do not be afraid," it said; "hold on tight, and you shall not go off till you are ready."

5. So the leaf stopped sighing, and went on singing and rustling. It grew all the summer long till October. And when the bright days of autumn came, the leaf saw all the leaves around growing very beautiful.

6. Some were yellow, some were brown, and many were striped with different colors. Then the leaf asked the tree what this meant.

7. The tree said, "All these leaves are getting ready to fly away, and they have put on these colors because of their joy."

8. Then the little leaf began to want to go, and grew very beautiful in thinking of it. When it was gay in colors, it saw that the branches of the tree had no bright colors on them.

9. So the leaf said, "O branch! why are you lead-colored while we are all beautiful and golden?"

10. "We must keep on our working clothes," said the tree, "for our work is not yet done; but your clothes are for holidays, because your task is now over."

11. Just then a little puff of wind came, and the leaf let go without thinking, and the wind took it up and turned it over and over.

12. Then it fell gently down under the edge of the fence, among hundreds of leaves, and has never waked to tell us what it dreamed about.

LESSON XLIII.

gōld	lămbṣ	fŏnd′ly	erĭck′et	whȋrl′ing
fȋeldṣ	lēaveṣ	flēe′çy	fâre′wĕll	eòv′er let
glāde	vāle	drēam	eon tĕnt′	flŭt′ter ing

THE WIND AND THE LEAVES.

1.

"Come, little leaves," said the wind one day.
"Come o'er the meadows with me, and play;
Put on your dress of red and gold,—
Summer is gone, and the days grow cold."

2.

Soon as the leaves heard the wind's loud call,
Down they came fluttering, one and all;
Over the brown fields they danced and **flew,**
Singing the soft little songs they knew.

3.

"Cricket, good-by, we've been friends so long;
Little brook, sing us your farewell song,—
Say you are sorry to see us go;
Ah! you will miss us, right well we know.

4.

"Dear little lambs, in your fleecy fold,
Mother will keep you from harm and cold;
Fondly we've watched you in vale and glade;
Say, will you dream of our loving shade?"

5.

Dancing and whirling, the little leaves went;
Winter had called them, and they were content.
Soon fast asleep in their earthy beds,
The snow laid a coverlet over their heads.

George Cooper.

LESSON XLIV.

wŏre	ḡrēen	jōke	Jĕs'sie	prĕṣ'ents
jŏl'ly	dēal	trĭm	ex pĕet'	lĕḡ'ḡingṣ

MAMMA'S PRESENT.

1. Jessie played a good joke on her mamma. This is the way she did it.

2. Jessie had gone to the woods with Jamie and Joe to get green branches to trim up the house for Christmas. She wore her little cap, her white furs, and her red leggings.

3. She was a merry little girl, indeed; but she felt sad this morning because her mother had said, "The children will all have Christmas presents, but I don't expect any for myself. We are too poor this year."

4. When Jessie told her brothers this, they all talked about it a great deal. "Such a good, kind mamma, and no Christmas present! It's too bad."

5. "I do n't like it," said little Jessie, with a tear in her eye.

6. "Oh, she has you," said Joe.

7. "But I am not something new," said Jessie.

8. "Well, you will be new, Jessie," said Joe, "when you get back. She has not seen you for an hour."

9. Jessie jumped and laughed. "Then put me in the basket, and carry me to mamma, and say, 'I am her Christmas present.'"

10. So they set her in the basket, and put green branches all around her. It was a jolly ride. They set her down on the doorstep, and went in and said, "There's a Christmas present out there for you, mamma."

11. Mamma went and looked, and there, in a basket of green branches, sat her own little laughing girl.

12. "Just the very thing I wanted most," said mamma.

13. "Then, dear mamma," said Jessie, bounding out of her leafy nest, " I

should think it would be Christmas for mammas all the time, for they see their little girls every day."

LESSON XLV.

pûr'ple   plūmeş
pāil   hăp'pened
eōat   shăl'lōw
wād'ed   Chärleş
năp   yĕs'ter daȳ

MARY'S STORY.

1. Father, and Charles, and Lucy, and I went to the beach yesterday. We took our dinner, and stayed all day.

2. 7

2. Father and Charles went out a little way from the shore in a boat, and fished, while Lucy and I gathered sea mosses.

3. We took off our shoes and stockings, and waded into the shallow water. We had a pail to put our seaweeds in.

4. We found such beautiful ones. Some were purple, some pink, and some brown. When they were spread out in the water, the purple ones looked like plumes, and the brown ones like little trees.

5. Such a funny thing happened to Lucy. She slipped on a stone, and down she went into the water. How we both laughed! But the wind and sun soon dried Lucy's dress.

6. Then father came and took us in the boat for a row. After that we had a picnic dinner in the woods.

7. Then father spread his coat on the grass, and took a nap while we children played on the beach.

LESSON XLVI.

bĭd	sŏre	smīle	Rălph	for ğĕt′
hāy	stĕm	shōne	Wĭck	se+rēam
tōre	point	plŭck	thôrnş	snătched

RALPH WICK.

1. Ralph Wick was seven years old. In most things he was a fine boy, but he was too apt to cry.

2. When he could not have what he wanted, he would cry for it and say, "I will have it."

3. If he was told that it would hurt him, and he could not have it, he would begin to tease and cry.

4. One day, he went with his mother into the fields. The sun shone. The grass was cut. The flowers were in bloom.

5. Ralph thought he was, for once, a good boy. A smile was on his face. He wished to do as he was told.

6. He said, "Mother, I will be good now. I will do as you bid me. Please let me toss this hay."

7. "That I will," said his mother. So they threw the hay, as Ralph wished, and he was very happy.

8. "Now you must be tired," said his mother. "Sit down here, and I will get a nice red rose for you."

9. "I would like to have one," said Ralph. So his mother brought the red rose to him.

10. "Thank you, mother," he said. "But you have a white one, also. Please give me that."

11. "No, my dear," said his mother. "See how many thorns it has on its stem. You must not touch it. If you should try to pluck a rose like this, you would be sure to hurt your hand."

12. When Ralph found that he could not have the white rose, he began to scream, and snatched it. But he was soon very sorry. The thorns tore his hand. It was so sore he could not use it for some time.

13. Ralph did not soon forget this. When he wanted what he should not have, his mother would point to his sore hand. He at last learned to do as he was told.

LESSON XLVII.

COASTING DOWN THE HILL.

slōpe	voiç'eş	rŭsh'ing	bēam'ing
trăck	chēeks	flŏod'ing	läugh'ter
hĕalth	a ḡlōw'	eōast'ing	trŭdġ'ing
frŏst'y	Iş'a bĕl	plĕaş'ure	lănd'seāpe

Frosty is the morning;
　　But the sun is bright,
Flooding all the landscape
　　With its golden light.
Hark the sounds of laughter
　　And of voices shrill!
See the happy children
　　Coasting down the hill!

There are Tom and Charley,
　　And their sister Nell;
There are John and Willie,
　　Kate and Isabel,—
Eyes with pleasure beaming,
　　Cheeks with health aglow;
Bless the merry children,
　　Trudging through the snow!

Now I hear them shouting,
"Ready! Clear the track"!
Down the slope they're rushing;
Now they're trotting back.
Full of fun and frolic,
Thus they come and go,
Coasting down the hillside,
Trudging through the snow.

LESSON XLVIII.

| hēed | sīght | slȳ'ly | strēam | drīft'ing |
| flŏck | flīght | snăps | hĭd'den | çīr'eling |

THE FOX AND THE DUCKS.

1. On a summer day, a man sitting on the bank of a river, in the shade of some bushes, watched a flock of ducks on the stream.

2. Soon a branch with leaves came drifting among them, and they all took

wing. After circling in the air for a little time, they settled down again on their feeding ground.

3. Soon another branch came drifting down among them, and again they took flight from the river; but when they found the branch had drifted by and done them no harm, they flew down to the water as before.

4. After four or five branches had drifted by in this way, the ducks gave little heed to them. At length, they hardly tried to fly out of their way,

even when the branches nearly touched them.

5. The man who had been watching all this, now began to wonder who had set these branches adrift. He looked up the stream, and spied a fox slyly watching the ducks. "What will he do next?" thought the man.

6. When the fox saw that the ducks were no longer afraid of the branches, he took a much larger branch than any he had yet used, and stretched himself upon it so as to be almost hidden. Then he set it afloat as he had the others.

7. Right among the flock drifted the sly old fox, and, making quick snaps to right and left, he seized two fine young ducks, and floated off with them.

8. The rest of the flock flew away in fright, and did not come back for a long time.

9. The fox must have had a fine dinner to pay him for his cunning, patient work.

LESSON XLIX.

sāint	sĭlk'en	sĭm'ple	pŏv'er ty
plāin	sĭn'ner	spĭn'ner	splĕn'dor
wõrth	stĕad'y	mûr'der	plăn'ning
sĭl'ver	tĕn'der	prŏv'erb	re mĕm'ber

PRETTY IS THAT PRETTY DOES.

1. The spider wears a plain brown dress,
   And she is a steady spinner;
To see her, quiet as a mouse,
   Going about her silver house,
You would never, never, never guess
   The way she gets her dinner.

2. She looks as if no thought of ill
   In all her life had stirred her;
But while she moves with careful tread,
And while she spins her silken thread,
She is planning, planning, planning still
   The way to do some murder.

3. My child, who reads this simple lay,
   With eyes down-dropt and tender,
Remember the old proverb says
That pretty is which pretty does,
And that worth does not go nor stay
   For poverty nor splendor.

4. 'T is not the house, and not the dress,
   That makes the saint or sinner.
To see the spider sit and spin,
Shut with her walls of silver in,
You would never, never, never guess
   The way she gets her dinner.

Alice Cary.

LESSON L.

çĭv'il	Pē'ter	Tow'şer	ap pēar'
a lōne'	Pĭn'dar	pẽr'sonş	trăv'el erş

THE STORY-TELLER.

1. Peter Pindar was a great story-teller. One day, as he was going by the school, the children gathered around him.

2. They said, "Please tell us a story we have never heard." Ned said, "Tell us something about boys and dogs."

3. " Well," said Peter, " I love to please good children, and, as you all appear civil, I will tell you a new story; and it shall be about a boy and some dogs, as Ned asks.

4. " But before we begin, let us sit down in a cool, shady place. And now, John, you must be as still as a little mouse. Mary, you must not let Towser bark nor make a noise.

5. "A long way from this place, there is a land where it is very cold, and much snow falls.

6. "The hills are very high there, and travelers are often lost among them. There are men there who keep large dogs. These are taught to hunt for people lost in the snow.

7. " The dogs have so fine a scent, that they can find persons by that alone.

8. " Sometimes it is so dark, that they can not see anything. Those who are lost often lie hid in the snow-drifts."

LESSON LI.

lāin   wēak
stiff   shrĭll
rōde   blēak

THE STORY-TELLER.

(CONCLUDED.)

1. "One cold, bleak night, the snow fell fast, and the wind blew loud and shrill. It was quite dark. Not a star was to be seen in the sky.

2. "These good men sent out a dog, to hunt for those who might want help.

In an hour or two, the dog was heard coming back.

3. "On looking out, they saw him with a boy on his back. The poor child was stiff with cold. He could but just hold on to the dog's back.

4. "He had lain for a long time in the snow, and was too weak to walk.

5. "He felt something pull him by the coat, and heard the bark of a dog. He put out his hand, and felt the dog. The dog gave him another pull.

6. "This gave the poor boy some hope, and he took hold of the dog. He drew himself out of the snow, but he could not stand or walk.

7. "He got on the dog's back, and put his arms round the dog's neck, and held on. He felt sure that the dog did not mean to do him any harm.

8. "Thus he rode all the way to the good men's house.

9. "They took care of him, till the snow was gone. Then they sent him to his home."

LESSON LII.

ōak	dŭsk	fīght	squēak	rŭf'fled
băḡ	Frĕd	whōō	a wāke'	erēep'ing

THE OWL.

1. " Where did you get that owl, Harry ? "

2. " Fred and I found him in the old, hollow oak."

3. " How did you know he was there ? "

4. " I'll tell you. Fred and I were playing 'hide and seek' round the old barn, one night just at dusk.

5. " I was just creeping round the corner, when I heard a loud squeak, and a big bird flew up with something in his claws.

6. " I called Fred, and we watched him as he flew to the woods. Fred thought the bird was an owl, and that he had a nest in the old oak.

7. " The next day we went to look

2, 8.

for him, and, sure enough, he was there."

8. "But how did you catch him? I should think he could fight like a good fellow with that sharp bill."

9. "He can when he is wide awake; but owls can't see very well in the daytime, and he was taking a nap.

10. "He opened his great eyes, and ruffled up his feathers, and said, 'Whoo! Whoo!' 'Never mind who,' Fred said, and slipped him into a bag."

LESSON LIII.

whōle	bōneṣ	seârçe'ly	mouṣ'er
mīçe	rōlled	sur prīṣe'	swal'lowṣ
wĭnk'ing	eŏm'ie al	dŭck'lingṣ	eăp'ture

THE OWL.
(CONCLUDED.)

1. "What are you going to do with him, Harry?"

2. "Let him go. He does n't like this cage half so well as his old oak tree. A young owl can be tamed easily, but this one is too old to tame."

3. "But won't he catch all your ducklings and little chickens?"

4. "No, not while there are any rats or mice around. Father says an owl is a good mouser, and can catch more mice than half a dozen cats."

5. "I'm glad I had a look at him before you let him go. What soft feathers he has!"

6. "Yes, he can fly so softly that

you can scarcely hear him, and for this reason he can easily surprise and capture his prey."

7. "How comical he looks, winking his big eyes slowly, and turning his head from side to side!"

8. "Yes; he is watching your dog. Be still, Bounce!

9. "We have just found out a funny thing about his way of eating. He breaks the bones of a mouse, and then swallows it whole. After an hour or two, he throws up the bones and fur rolled up in a little ball."

LESSON LIV.

broad   knēe

fĭḡ   frĕsh

çĭt′y   trout

ŭn der nēath′

fought (fawt)

sur prīṣed′

-elăp′ping

gär′den

eăr′ry ing

fīght′ing

GRANDFATHER'S STORY.

1. "Come and sit by my knee, Jane, and grandfather will tell you a strange story.

2. "One bright summer day, I was in a garden in a city, with a friend. We rested underneath a fig tree. The broad leaves were green and fresh.

3. "We looked up at the ripe, purple figs. And what do you think came down through the branches of the fig tree over our heads?"

4. "Oh, a bird, grandfather, a bird!" said little Jane, clapping her hands.

5. "No, not a bird. It was a fish; a trout, my little girl."

6. "Not a fish, grandfather! A trout come through the branches of a tree in the city? I am sure you must be in fun."

7. "No, Jane, I tell you the truth. My friend and I were very much surprised to see a fish falling from a fig tree.

8. "But we ran from under the tree, and saw a fishhawk flying, and an eagle after him.

9. "The hawk had caught the fish, and was carrying it home to his nest, when the eagle saw it and wanted it.

10. "They fought for it. The fish was dropped, and they both lost it. So much for fighting!"

LESSON LV.

flōw   wīde   stēep   lākes   twĭn'kling

GOD IS GREAT AND GOOD.

1. I know God made the sun
   To fill the day with light;
He made the twinkling stars
   To shine all through the night.

2. He made the hills that rise
   So very high and steep;

He made the lakes and seas,
That are so broad and deep.

3. He made the streams so wide,
That flow through wood and vale;
He made the rills so small,
That leap down hill and dale.

4. He made each bird that sings
So sweetly all the day;
He made each flower that springs
So bright, so fresh, so gay.

5. And He who made all these,
He made both you and me;
Oh, let us thank Him, then,
For great and good is He.

LESSON LVI.

hōe	ḡrāve	knŏck	ex çĕpt′
drōll	hy̆mn	prāyed	eŏt′tag̣e

A GOOD OLD MAN.

1. There once lived an old man in a snug, little cottage. It had two rooms and only two windows. A small garden lay just behind it.

2. Old as the poor man was, he used to work in the fields. Often he would come home very tired and weak, with his hoe or spade on his shoulder.

3. And who do you think met him at the door? Mary and Jane, his two little grandchildren.

4. They were too young to work, except to weed in the garden, or bring water from the spring.

5. In winter, as they were too poor to buy much wood or coal, they had little fire; so they used to sit close together to keep warm. Mary would sit on one of the old man's knees, and Jane on the other.

6. Sometimes their grandfather would tell them a droll story. Sometimes he would teach them a hymn.

7. He would often talk to them of their father, who had gone to sea, or of their good, kind mother, who was in her grave. Every night he prayed God to bless them, and to bring back their father in safety.

8. The old man grew weaker every year; but the little girls were glad to work for him, who had been so good to them.

9. One cold, windy night, they heard a knock at the door. The little girls ran and opened it. Oh, joy to them! There stood their father.

10. He had been at sea a long time. He had saved some money, and had now come home to stay.

11. After this the old man did not have to work. His son worked for him, and his grandchildren took care of him. Many happy days they spent together.

dīned	ḡāy′ly	dŏe′tor	ḡlŭt′ton
nēedṣ	līve′ly	ā′ɛornṣ	rĕad′erṣ
tāstes	La̤u′rȧ	ḡrēed′y	tĕm′perṣ

THE GREEDY GIRL.

aura English is a greedy little girl. Indeed, she is quite a glutton. Do you know what a glutton is? A glutton is one who eats too much, because the food tastes well.

2. Laura's mother is always willing she should have as much to eat as is good for her; but sometimes, when her mother is not watching, she eats so much that it makes her sick.

3. I do not know why she is so silly. Her kitten never eats more than it needs. It leaves the nice bones on the plate, and lies down to sleep when it has eaten enough.

4. The bee is wiser than Laura. It

flies all day among the flowers to gather honey, and might eat the whole time if it pleased. But it eats just enough, and carries all the rest to its hive.

5. The squirrel eats a few nuts or acorns, and frisks about as gayly as if he had dined at the king's table.

6. Did you ever see a squirrel with a nut in his paws? How bright and lively he looks as he eats it!

7. If he lived in a house made of acorns, he would never need a doctor. He would not eat an acorn too much.

8. I do not love little girls who eat too much. Do you, my little readers?

9. I do not think they have such rosy cheeks, or such bright eyes, or such sweet, happy tempers as those who eat less.

LESSON LVIII.

lĕnd	Sā'rah	ċȯm'fort	a shāmed'
yọurṣ	wĭll'ing	thĭm'ble	ĕlse'whêre
ūṣ'ing	bŏr'row	of fĕnd'ed	de pĕnd'ed

A PLACE FOR EVERYTHING.

Mary. I wish you would lend me your thimble, Sarah. I can never find my own.

Sarah. Why is it, Mary, you can never find it?

Mary. How can I tell? But if you will not lend me yours, I can borrow one elsewhere.

Sarah. I am willing to lend mine to you, Mary. But I would very much like to know why you come to me to borrow so often.

Mary. Because you never lose any of your things, and always know where to find them.

Sarah. And why do I always know where to find my things?

Mary. I do not know why, I am sure. If I did know, I might sometimes find my own.

Sarah. I will tell you the secret. I have a place for everything, and I put everything in its place when I have done using it.

Mary. O Sarah! who wants to run and put away a thing as soon as she has used it, as if her life depended upon it?

Sarah. Our life does not depend upon it, but our comfort does, surely. How much more time will it take to put a thing in its place, than to hunt for it or to borrow whenever you want to use it?

Mary. Well, Sarah, I will never borrow of you again, you may depend upon it.

Sarah. You are not offended with me, I hope.

Mary. No, but I am ashamed. Before night, I will have a place for everything, and then I will keep everything in its place. You have taught me a lesson that I shall remember.

LESSON LIX.

eŏn'stant

ēar

dĭdst

härk

nŏne

thīne

ēaṣe

re joiçe'

lēad'ing

lŭll

mēek

thēe

mīld

nûrse

thȳ

frĕt'fụl

MY MOTHER.

Hark! my mother's voice I hear.
Sweet that voice is to my ear;
Ever soft, it seems to tell,
Dearest child, I love thee well.

2, 9.

Love me, mother? Yes, I know
None can love so well as thou.
Was it not upon thy breast
I was taught to sleep and rest?

Didst thou not, in hours of pain,
Lull this head to ease again?
With the music of thy voice,
Bid my little heart rejoice?

Ever gentle, meek, and mild,
Thou didst nurse thy fretful child.
Teach these little feet the road
Leading on to heaven and God.

What return then can I make?
This fond heart, dear mother, take;
Thine it is, in word and thought,
Thine by constant kindness bought.

LESSON LX.

skĭp′ping   mēan   Geôrġe   ġĭft

en ġāġed′   Mā′son   El′let

THE BROKEN WINDOW.

1. George Ellet had a bright silver dollar for a New-year gift.

2. He thought of all the fine things he might buy with it.

3. The ground was all covered with snow; but the sun shone out bright, and everything looked beautiful.

4. So George put on his hat, and ran into the street. As he went skipping along, he met some boys throwing snowballs. George soon engaged in the sport.

5. He sent a ball at James Mason, but it missed him, and broke a window on the other side of the street.

6. George feared some one would come out of the house and find him. So he ran off as fast as he could.

7. As soon as he got round the next corner, George stopped, because he was very sorry for what he had done.

8. He said to himself, "I have no right to spend my silver dollar, now. I ought to go back, and pay for the glass I broke with my snowball."

9. He went up and down the street, and felt very sad. He wished very much to buy something nice. He also wished to pay for the broken glass.

10. At last he said, "It was wrong to break the window, though I did not mean to do it. I will go and pay for it, if it takes all my money. I will try not to be sorry. I do not think the man will hurt me if I pay for the mischief I have done."

LESSON LXI.

| mẽr′chant | hŏn′est ly | răng | mīnd |
| pärt′ner | with out′ | rĭch | bĕll |

THE BROKEN WINDOW.

(CONCLUDED.)

1. George started off, and felt much happier for having made up his mind to do what was right.

2. He rang the doorbell. When the man came out, George said, "Sir, I

threw a snowball through your window. But I did not intend to do it. I am very sorry, and wish to pay you. Here is the dollar my father gave me as a New-year gift."

3. The gentleman took the dollar, and asked George if he had no more money. George said he had not. " Well," said he, "this will do."

4. So, after asking George his name, and where he lived, he called him an honest boy, and shut the door.

5. George went home at dinner time, with a face as rosy, and eyes as bright, as if nothing had gone wrong. At dinner, Mr. Ellet asked him what he had bought with his money.

6. George very honestly told him all about the broken window, and said he felt very well without any money to spend.

7. When dinner was over, Mr. Ellet told George to go and look in his cap. He did so, and found two silver dollars there.

8. The man, whose window had been broken, had been there, and told Mr. Ellet about it. He gave back George's dollar and another besides.

9. A short time after this, the man came and told Mr. Ellet that he wanted a good boy to stay in his store.

10. As soon as George left school, he went to live with this man, who was a rich merchant. In a few years he became the merchant's partner.

LESSON LXII.

līne	fĭḡ'ūre	sĕe'ond	pẽr'feet ly
ḡrāin	vĕrse	ad vīçe'	im pā'tient
stŭd'y	buṣ'i ly	fŏl'lowed	ŭn der stănd'

FRANK AND THE HOURGLASS.

1. Frank was a very talkative little boy. He never saw a new thing without asking a great many questions about it.

2. His mother was very patient and

kind. When it was proper to answer his questions, she would do so.

3. Sometimes she would say, "You are not old enough to understand that, my son. When you are ten years old, you may ask me about it, and I will tell you."

4. When his mother said this, he never teased any more. He knew she always liked to answer him when he asked proper questions.

5. The first time Frank saw an hourglass, he was very much amused; but he did not know what it was.

6. His mother said, "An hourglass is made in the shape of the figure 8. The sand is put in at one end, and runs through a small hole in the middle. As much sand is put into the glass as will run through in an hour."

7. Frank watched the little stream of sand. He was impatient, because it would not run faster. "Let me shake it, mother," said he; "it is lazy, and will never get through."

8. "Oh yes, it will, my son," said his mother. "The sand moves by little and little, but it moves all the time.

9. "When you look at the hands of the clock, you think they go very slowly, and so they do; but they never stop.

10. "While you are at play the sand is running, grain by grain. The hands of the clock are moving, second by second.

11. "At night, the sand in the hour-glass has run through twelve times. The hour hand of the clock has moved all round its great face.

12. "This is because they keep at work every minute. They do not stop to think how much they have to do, and how long it will take them to do it."

13. Now, Frank's mother wanted him to learn a little hymn; but he said, "Mother, I can never learn it."

14. His mother said, "Study all the time. Never stop to ask how long it

will take to learn it. You will be able
to say it very soon."

15. Frank followed his mother's ad-
vice. He studied line after line, very
busily; and in one hour and a half he
knew the hymn perfectly.

LESSON LXIII.

sleet chēer'ly erṳ'el tăps frēe

MARCH.

1. In the snowing and the blowing,
    In the cruel sleet,
Little flowers begin their growing
    Far beneath our feet.

2. Softly taps the Spring, and cheerly,—
"Darlings, are you here?"
Till they answer, "We are nearly,
Nearly ready, dear."

3. "Where is Winter, with his snowing?
Tell us, Spring," they say.
Then she answers, "He is going,
Going on his way.

4. "Poor old Winter does not love you;
But his time is past;
Soon my birds shall sing above you;—
Set you free at last."

Mary Mapes Dodge.

LESSON LXIV.

lāte	strạw	Jĕn'ny	snôrt'ed	Tĕm'plar
äunt	rōḡue	re pōrt'	ḡrāz'ing	di rĕet'ly
dĭtch	ăet'ed	sĕrv'içe	sup pōṣe'	ea rĕssed'
hīred	e rĕet'	prĭcked	mŏ'ment	ḡrō'çer ĭeṣ

JENNY'S CALL.

1. "It's of no use, Mrs. Templar; I have been trying the greater part of an hour

to catch that rogue of a horse. She won't be caught."

2. Such was the report the hired man brought in to Mrs. Templar one pleasant May morning, when she had been planning a ride.

3. "I suppose it can not be helped, but I wanted her very much," she said, as she turned away.

4. "What was it you wanted, mother?" asked Jenny Templar, a bright, brown-haired, brown-eyed girl of twelve, who had just come into the room.

5. "Fanny," said the mother. "It is such a beautiful morning, I meant to drive down to the village, get some groceries, then call for your Aunt Ann, have a nice ride up the river road, and bring her home to dinner.

6. "But father is away for all day, and the men have been trying nearly an hour to catch Fanny; one of the men says she can't be caught."

7. "Maybe she can't by him," said Jenny, with a merry laugh. "But, get ready, mother; you shall go if you like. I'll catch Fanny, and harness her, too."

8. "Why, my child, they say she jumped the ditch three or four times, and acted like a wild creature. You'll only be late at school, and tire yourself for nothing."

9. "It won't take me long, mother. Fanny will come to me," said Jenny, cheerily. She put on her wide straw hat, and was off in a moment, down the hill, to the field where the horse was grazing.

10. The moment Fanny heard the rustle of Jenny's dress, she pricked up her ears, snorted, and, with head erect, seemed ready to bound away again.

11. "Fanny! O Fanny!" called Jenny, and the beautiful creature turned her head. That gentle tone she well knew, and, glad to see her friend, she came directly to the fence, and rubbed her head on the girl's shoulder. As soon as the gate was opened, she followed Jenny to the barn.

12. The men had treated her roughly, and she remembered it. But she knew

and loved the voice that was always kind, and the hand that often fed and caressed her. She gave love for love, and willing service for kindness.

LESSON LXV.

rŭng Dā′vy vī′o lĕt re çĕss′ ar rānġe′
fĕrns mä′ple dāin′ty lĭn′ġered pret′ti est

POOR DAVY.

1. It was recess time at the village school. The bell had rung, and the children had run out into the bright sunshine, wild with laughter and fun.

2. All but poor Davy. He came out last and very slowly, but he did not laugh. He was in trouble, and the bright, golden sunlight did not make him glad.

3. He walked across the yard, and sat down on a stone behind the old maple. A little bird on the highest branch sang just to make him laugh.

4. But Davy did not notice it. He was thinking of the cruel words that had been said about his ragged clothes. The tears stole out of his eyes, and ran down his cheeks.

5. Poor Davy had no father, and his mother had to work hard to keep him at school.

6. That night, he went home by the path that led across the fields and through the woods. He still felt sad.

2, 10.

7. Davy did not wish to trouble his mother; so he lingered a while among the trees, and at last threw himself on the green moss under them.

8. Just then his teacher came along. She saw who it was, and stopped, saying kindly, "What is the matter, Davy?"

9. He did not speak, but the tears began again to start.

10. "Won't you tell me? Perhaps I can help you."

11. Then he told her all his trouble. When he ended, she said, cheerily, "I have a plan, Davy, that I think will help you."

12. "Oh, what is it?" he said, sitting up with a look of hope, while a tear fell upon a blue violet.

13. "Well, how would you like to be a little flower merchant?"

14. "And earn money?" said Davy. "That would be jolly. But where shall I get my flowers?"

15. "Right in these woods, and in the fields," said his teacher. "Here are lovely blue violets, down by the brook are white ones, and among the rocks are ferns and mosses. Bring them all to my house, and I will help you arrange them."

16. So, day after day, Davy hunted the woods for the prettiest flowers, and the most dainty ferns and mosses. After his teacher had helped to arrange them, he took them to the city that was near, and sold them.

17. He soon earned money enough to buy new clothes. Now the sunshine and the bird's songs make him glad.

LESSON LXVI.

dēep	flour ·	dōugh	mĭll'er	whĕth'er
eŏŏk	a fär'	dŭst'y	erā'dleṣ	ḡrīnd'ing
ḡlōw	dȯth	văl'ley	rēap'erṣ	a-knēad'ing

ALICE'S SUPPER.

1.

Far down in the valley the wheat grows deep,
And the reapers are making the cradles sweep;
And this is the song that I hear them sing,
While cheery and loud their voices ring:
" 'T is the finest wheat that ever did grow!
And it is for Alice's supper—ho! ho!"

2.

Far down by the river the old mill stands,
And the miller is rubbing his dusty hands;
And these are the words of the miller's lay,
As he watches the millstones grinding away:
" 'T is the finest flour that money can buy,
And it is for Alice's supper—hi! hi!"

3.

Downstairs in the kitchen the fire doth glow,
And cook is a-kneading the soft, white dough;
And this is the song she is singing to-day,
As merry and busy she's working away:
"'T is the finest dough, whether near or afar,
And it is for Alice's supper—ha! ha!"

4.

To the nursery now comes mother, at last,
And what in her hand is she bringing so fast?

'T is a plateful of something, all yellow and
 white,
And she sings as she comes, with her smile
 so bright:
" 'T is the best bread and butter I ever did see,
And it is for Alice's supper—he! he!"

LESSON LXVII.

tạll	hŭng	stôrm	pĭck'et
fīrṣ	nôrth	ḡownṣ	spär'kled
rōōf	flākes	fâir'ieṣ	ċăp'taĭnṣ

A SNOWSTORM.

1. Last night, the cold north wind
blew great snow clouds over the sky.
Not a star, not a bit of blue sky could
be seen.

2. Soon the tiny flakes floated softly
down, like flocks of little white birds.
Faster and faster they came, till they
filled the air. They made no noise, but
they were busy all night long.

3. They covered all the ground with
a soft, white carpet. They hung beauti-

ful plumes on the tall, green firs. The
little bushes, they put to sleep in warm
nightgowns and caps.

4. They hid the paths so that the
boys might have the fun of digging
new ones. They turned the old picket
fence into a row of soldiers, and the
gate posts into captains, with tall white
hats on.

5. The old corn basket that was left out by the barn, upside down, they made into a cunning little snow house with a round roof.

6. When the busy little flakes had done their work, the sun came up to see what they had been about.

7. He must have been pleased with what he saw, for .he smiled such a bright, sweet smile, that the whole white world sparkled as if it were made of little stars.

8. Who would have thought that the black clouds could hide the little fairies that made the earth so beautiful!

LESSON LXVIII.

dŭḡ	rōōts	thŭmp	of fĕnse'
tōad	spōōlṣ	hēaped	smōōthed
fōrth	ā'pron	clŏṣ'ets	dăn'de lī onṣ

BESSIE.

1. One day, Bessie thought how nice it would be to have a garden with only

wild flowers in it. So into the house she ran to find her Aunt Annie, and ask her leave to go over on the shady hillside, across the brook, where the wild flowers grew thickest.

2. "Yes, indeed, you may go," said Aunt Annie; "but what will you put the roots and earth in while you are making the garden?"

3. "Oh," said Bessie, "I can take my apron."

4. Her aunt laughed, and said, "A basket will be better, I think." So they looked in the closets and the attic, everywhere; but some of the baskets were full, and some broken; not one could they find that would do.

5. Then Aunt Annie turned out the spools and the bags from a nice large workbasket, and gave that to Bessie. "You may have this for your own," she said, "to fill with earth, or flowers, or anything you like."

6. "Oh! thank you," said Bessie, and she danced away through the garden. She slipped through the gate, out into the field all starred with dandelions, down in the hollow by the brook, then up on the hillside out of sight among the shady trees.

7. How she worked that afternoon! She heaped up the dark, rich earth, and smoothed it over with her hands. Then she dug up violets, and spring-beauties, and other flowers,—running back and forth, singing all the while.

8. The squirrels peeped out of their holes at Bessie. The birds sang in the branches overhead. Thump, came something all at once into the middle of the bed. Bessie jumped and upset the basket, and away it rolled down the hill.

9. How Bessie laughed when she saw a big, brown toad winking his bright eyes at her, as if he would say, " No offense, I hope."

10. Just then Bessie heard a bell ringing loudly. She knew it was calling her home; but how could she leave her basket? She must look for that first.

11. " Waiting, waiting, waiting," all at once sang a bird out of sight among the branches; "waiting, Bessie."

12. " Sure enough," said Bessie; " perhaps I'm making dear mother or auntie wait; and they are so good to me. I'd better let the basket wait. Take care of it, birdie; and don't jump on my flowers, Mr. Toad."

LESSON LXIX.

vĭṣ'it   sōaked   o bē'di ent   rụ'ined

B E S S I E.
(CONCLUDED.)

1. She was back at the house in a few minutes, calling, "Mother! mother! auntie! Who wants me?"

2. "I, dear," said her mother. "I am going away for a long visit, and if you had not come at once, I could not have said good-by to my little girl."

3. Then Bessie's mother kissed her, and told her to obey her kind aunt while she was gone.

4. The next morning, Bessie waked to find it raining hard. She went into her aunt's room with a very sad face. "O auntie! this old rain!"

5. "This new, fresh, beautiful rain, Bessie! How it will make our flowers grow, and what a good time we can have together in the house!"

6. "I know it, auntie; but you will think me so careless!"

7. "To let it rain?"

8. "No; do n't laugh, Aunt Annie; to leave your nice basket out of doors all night; and now it will be soaked and ruined in this——this——beautiful rain." Bessie did not look as if the beautiful rain made her very happy.

9. "You must be more careful, dear, another time," said her aunt, gently. "But come, tell me all about it."

10. So Bessie crept very close to her auntie's side, and told her of her happy

time the day before; of the squirrel, and the toad, and how the basket rolled away down the hill; and then how the bell rang, and she could not stop to find the basket.

11. "And you did quite right," said her aunt. "If you had stopped, your mother must have waited a whole day, or else gone without seeing you. When I write, I will tell her how obedient you were, and that will please her more than anything else I can say."

LESSON LXX.

sôught	sure'ly (shu̯)	wĕl'eome	light'sŏme
lŏft'y	māid'en	chĕr'ished	ĭn tro dūçe'

CHEERFULNESS.

There is a little maiden—
　Who is she? Do you know?
Who always has a welcome,
　Wherever she may go.

Her face is like the May time,
  Her voice is like a bird's;
The sweetest of all music
  Is in her lightsome words.

Each spot she makes the brighter,
  As if she were the sun;
And she is sought and cherished
  And loved by everyone;

By old folks and by children,
  By lofty and by low:
Who is this little maiden?
  Does anybody know?

You surely must have met her,
  You certainly can guess;
What! I must introduce her?
  Her name is Cheerfulness

Marian Douglas.

wĕst′ern　brēathe　dȳ′ing　mōon　bābe　sāilş

LULLABY.

1. Sweet and low, sweet and low,
   Wind of the western sea,
   Low, low, breathe and blow,
   Wind of the western sea!
   Over the rolling waters go,
   Come from the dying moon, and blow,
   Blow him again to me;
   While my little one, while my pretty one
   sleeps.

2. Sleep and rest, sleep and rest,
   Father will come to thee soon;
   Rest, rest, on mother's breast,
   Father will come to thee soon;
   Father will come to his babe in the nest,
   Silver sails all out of the west,
   Under the silver moon;
   Sleep, my little one, sleep, my pretty one,
   sleep.

Tennyson.

www.ingramcontent.com/pod-product-compliance
Lightning Source LLC
Chambersburg PA
CBHW070837100426
42813CB00003B/648